Notes
from the
universe

Book 3

**More from www.tut.com or
at bookstores everywhere:**

Dandelion,
The Extraordinary Life of a Misfit
Sheelagh Mawe, 1994

Totally Unique Thoughts,
Reminders of Life's Everyday Magic
Mike Dooley, 1998

Lost in Space
Mike Dooley, 1998

Thoughts Become Things * LIVE!
Audio Tape/CD, Mike Dooley, 2001

Infinite Possibilities:
The Art of Living Your Dreams
Audio Program, Mike Dooley, 2002

Notes from the Universe, Book 1 & 2
Mike Dooley, 2003 & 2005

The Most Important Lesson of All
Audio CD, Sheelagh Mawe & Andy Dooley, 2003

Notes from the Universe
Screensaver Software, Greeting Cards, Calendars, etc.

Notes from the universe

Book 3

new
perspectives
from an
old friend

Mike Dooley

TOTALLY UNIQUE THOUGHTS®

For Dad

Foreword

Can you imagine an astral plane somewhere "out there" where very old souls could rendezvous to practice and perfect their most highly developed manifestation techniques? A members-only kind of place, where whatever they think about comes to life in the most vivid high definition, surround sound, Technicolor, vis-à-vis the most intricate plots and circumstances? Where the only limits that exist lie in their ability to imagine what they have never before imagined, and to move with it in anticipation of its "physical" expression?

And best of all, being astral, no harm can come to them. They're completely untouchable. Nothing is real, yet everything matters. And there can be infinite gains in terms of insight and fun, yet no losses since everything is illusory. Actually, the worst thing that can happen is that they temporarily become so entranced by their creations, they completely forget who they are, where they are, and how powerful they really are.

Yep, it would be exactly like this astral plane. Only here, to help wake 'em up from their trance, we're experimenting with *Notes from the Universe...*

To clarify "eternal"

just a smidge...

Once the river of time has rounded her final bend,
and the last star in the sky has brightened its last
night, and every child who may ever be conceived
has been given ten thousand names,
we will have just begun.

Got time?

*When I think of how much you and I have to look
forward to, I could almost hyperventilate.*

Want to know what's better

than having it all? Way, way better?

Not having it all, but knowing of its inevitability, in a never-ending adventure that's just barely begun.

Yeeeeeehaaaaaaaaaaaaaaaaa!

Kind of like Friday is before the weekend.

It never fails to amaze me.

Create a paradise out of the ether. Throw in some wildlife, volcanoes, and wind storms. Some iguanas, koalas, and waterfalls. Come back a few billion years later and just when it looks like the whole place is going to implode - with pollution, disease, and war; famine, fatigue and fright - *there are still those* who see the beauty. Who act with kindness. And who live with hope and gratitude.

Actually, they carry the entire planet.

Who'd have thunk?

Yeah, OK. Guilty.

Do you know
what "unlimited" means?

It means you decide — *everything.*

Without a doubt

right here and now, as you read these very words
with eyes that sparkle, this golden day, amid your
dancing manifestations in a perfect world on an
emerald planet while your heart beats, your blood
flows, and angels peer over your shoulder, I think
you just might be the luckiest person alive.

There's no predicament

that can't be turned into an advantage. No foe
who can't become a friend, and no burden that
cannot give you wings.

How fair is that?

Ain't it grand?

Doesn't it boggle your mind? The harmony, the splendor, the beauty. The intricacies, the synchronicities, the staggering perfection. Do you ever wonder how it all came about?

Do you think I studied quarks, atoms, and molecules? That I drew schematics for the sun, the moon, and the stars; the otter, the Gila Monster, and the penguin? Do you think I painted every zebra, flower, and butterfly?

Or, do you think I simply imagined the end result?

Yep. The latter.

Now that's what I'm talking about.

And it's all you ever have to do.

Sheez, I thought you knew I hated school.

Do you think you're going to feel

cheated on the day you discover that your
countless successes were pretty much inevitable?
And that all the doubts, the fretting, and the
worries were a silly waste of time? Or do you
think you'll just roll with things... carefree...
blissful... and with a permanent cat-like
smile on your face?

Yeah. Roll, and the other stuff. That's what we
said you'd do.

So... how about it?

A-one, and a-two...
Meow, meow, meow, meow...
Meow, meow, meow, meow,
the Universe, and all her proud felines

To set the record straight:

However cool you think it might be to have an Out-of-Body experience - floating over your house, flying through space, traversing the past, present and future - let me tell you, it'll never be as cool as being in the one you now have. Walking barefoot in the grass, floating on a sun drenched pool, or even dancing alone in the dark.

You so "fly",
The Universe

Trust me, from here, getting In-To-Body is considered the most sacred of all sacreds.

I hope you're loving your life.
And I do mean really, really loving your life.

Because right now, there are so many others who are (*loving your life*). Here, and in the unseen.

No, not all of them will admit it but I know these things, and one day they'll know them, too.

I gotta confess

every now and then, I get this incredible urge to splurge on myself. To really indulge. Pull out all the stops. And tickle every one of my senses.

Yep, and that's when I'll choose a lifetime like yours. With obstacles to challenge me, people to "test" me, and circumstances that force me to see things that even I have never seen before. And a personality like yours, that possesses faith so daring that even when lost, you still hope. Dreams so bold that even when you fall, you get back up. And a heart so big, that even when it breaks, as all big hearts do, there's always room for second chances and new romances.

That's what I do.

Talk about crazy, sexy and cool!
The Universe

Thanks.

Whoops... I did it again.

Took a little nap, had a few dreams, and worlds were born. Planets spun and cooled. Continents rose and fell. And civilizations clashed and united.

Actually, it's quite good fun. But I also dreamed I was you. And in that dream, for a spell, I didn't remember I was also the Universe.

It was frightful, actually. Just about scared me to death until, as you, I slowly remembered who I was. And in those waking moments it was as if the earth shook, the seas danced, and the skies rejoiced almost as much as myself. As if they were waking up too, and it was the most beautiful, sublime, intoxicating rush of pure joy, I think I've *ever* known.

How I wish I could tell you more. But like a farmer eager for the new crop, any rush to harvest would spoil the yield. Besides, words would utterly fail me.

The sad part

is that they told you it's wrong to be selfish, tacky
to be vain, vulgar to be sexy, and wasteful
to be rich.

The happy part, is that they were just
making all that up.

Probably just jealous of all you might do, be
and have. And afraid of all they might not.

Uh-oh... One of them is in trouble now, gotta bolt!

Sometimes, when what they said

or promised, doesn't match what they did. And what they did, to this day, still hurts. You're better off forgetting all about it... knowing that I won't.

I'm like an elephant.

OK, for just 5 minutes

forget the bucks. Forget your soul mate, too. Forget the new car, the "home run", and being on Oprah. Your fears, your problems, and your pain. And during those 5 minutes, just feel the feelings, you most want to feel, for the rest of your life.

It might seem awkward, that's OK. It might seem silly, too. And I can just about guarantee, at first, it'll feel utterly futile... until your entire life begins changing.

If I were a beggar, I'd beg you. If I prayed in question marks this is what I'd ask for. And if I could implore you to do anything, let this be it. Because *nothing else* that you might ever do will have as profound an affect on your fortunes, friendships, and happiness; in navigating the illusions, manifesting what you want, and avoiding what you dread; as this little 5 minute drill performed just once a day, as often as you remember to do it.

And just so you know, if you do this right now or even every day for the rest of your life, I'll add back those 5 minutes to each of the days you do it. I'll just sneak 'em in there, and they'll feel like 10. But... not a word to anyone.

And that reminds me,
since I don't pray in question marks,
I hope you don't either.

You know, "Can I, please...? Will you, please...? "If I do x, or sacrifice y, will you do z...?". We have spam filters here, too, and since only you can answer those kind of questions, they kind of just go in one port, and out the other.

But, hubba-hubba, if you pray in "thank yous", especially for stuff you haven't yet received or experienced but as if you already had, those we *all* hear.

Amen!
The Universe

It took some craftiness

to create the splendors you now live in, because it all had to be done with the most exquisite balance, and in just such a way that you'd never, ever become bored.

Yeah, I had to throw in a few valleys, so that you could truly appreciate the peaks. A few scaly, ugly, biting creatures, to make the others more adorable. Some slippery slopes, dangerous curves, and moving targets, to show you how agile, brilliant, and cunning you are. And some quicksand, tornadoes, and earthquakes, to help you appreciate a stolen nap, an evening stroll, and quiet times.

But perhaps, best of all, I had to dream up some pretty special people. You know, with perspectives and traits so unlike your own, that sometimes it would seem your only means of surviving the relationship, would be learning to love yourself, even more. Aren't they a piece of work?

Oh, the sublime irony,
The Universe

Phew... I need a break!

Tell you what, why don't you write your own NOTE today? To *me?*

You could say something like, "Jambo Universe, it's me! Right, the good looking, talented, sexy one for whom the sun rises everyday. Anyway, just wanted to tell you that this adventure in time and space has been awesome. Ev*erything* I had ever expected it would be. (Huh, imagine that). That it's been exactly as hard and as easy, as challenging and as rewarding, as I've been telling myself. (Hey, what a coincidence). And that even though I know we are ONE, I still like thinking of you "out there" somewhere, watching, loving and protecting me. (Hmmm, could this also be why I sometimes feel alone?). At any rate, I'm learning tons, having some fun, and really looking forward to coming home one day. (Unless, of course, I'm home now).

Hey, since I have your attention, thanks, for another day in paradise. (Where my thoughts become things, dreams never stop coming true, and it all just keeps getting better and better).

You never cease to amaze me.

Next time you feel *really* hurt,

really angry, or *really, really* upset, and you're sure that even I have been violated, shaken and humbled, quick check and see if the sky is any less blue, the sun any less radiant, the birds have stopped singing, or the flowers have lost their scent.

I'll wager you'll find that life has gone on much as before. Too consumed by the powers of now and the inevitabilities of love, understanding, and eternal life, to have even missed a beat.

Oh-wee-oh,
The Universe

That's if there even is a next time.

"Grasshopper"

you may not always know what your invisible,
limiting beliefs are. But you do always know the
kinds of empowering beliefs you'd like to possess.
And so, one decision at a time, one day at a time,
you can choose to behave accordingly. And
thereby effectively kick some wicked
limiting-belief-butt.

*For every decision, crossroads, or act of faith, choose
with the mind of the highest within you. Until that's all
there is.*

There's *always* another way.
Always.

It takes a really special person,
someone quite extraordinary, to find *true* happiness in the lap of luxury surrounded by wealth and abundance, friends and laughter, and choices, choices, choices.

And funnily enough, it's usually the exact same kind of person who could be happy without all that, spending time alone, maybe with a book, or some tools, or a dog for the odd distraction.

Get my drift?

Nothing you will ever do,

be or have, no matter how stunning and
spectacular, will ever compare to your
achievement of being here at all.

Yes, *your* achievement.

*Amazing though, how people will put off celebrating
the big stuff, for the little stuff.
Don't wait.*

There hasn't been one

single day of your life that the world hasn't been
made a better place by your mere presence in it.

If you only knew.

Just do what you can
with what's before you today...
and leave "spectacular" to me.

K?

*The same goes for "profound", "stellar",
"revolutionary", and "outrageous".*

Whatever you focus on,

you *will* experience.

So if you talk about "what is" or "what was", even if you're just explaining them to a friendly ear, you project more of the same into the future. If you ask more than you give thanks, you'll believe less in your own power. And if you insist that it's hard and that you're lonely, you can count on more of both.

It's so within you...

Whatever you focus on, you will experience.

It was such a sad, sad picture.
She cried and cried, and ever so faintly murmured,
"Oh, how I wish you were here with me now...
That you'd have always been with me...
That we could have lived forever."

And so I whispered into her ear so softly that my
words could only be felt, not heard,
"He is, he will be, and you do."

She'll see.

Never trust appearances.

Can you hear it?

The *entire* Kingdom now beckons.

There were no tests, no hoops, and no limits.

All I have, I press to you at this very moment.

This is all you have to know.

And all you have to do is make room for the torrent which will flow in direct proportion to your every preparation, including what you do today.

You mean the world to me.

You know, a kind word

can move mountains and change lives. But for those times when they've escaped you, when neither the right thing was said, nor at the right time, kind thoughts can do the same. And better, thoughts have a way of lingering, seeking, and finding their intended beneficiary, unfettered by time and space. So it's never too late to think 'em, nor are you ever too far away.

Just a little something a tree once told me.

Guess who's thinking of you, right now.

Has it occurred to you

that wherever you go, *you* are my eyes, my ears, and my voice; my arms, my legs, and my every-thing else, too?

Well, I vote for more flowers, more music, and more "I love you's". More hugging, more skipping, and more naps.

But that's just me.

xxxxxxxxxxxooooooooooooo!

TOGA! TOGA! TOGA!

What, just because it's Monday you don't think we party?

Believe me, here *it never ends!*

The homecoming parties are really crazy! Old loves and friendships are rekindled and spontaneous enlightenment is passed around like, well, like you know what. But then, there are the other parties... whoooweeee! Real hoedowns for the most brilliant, radiant, and illuminated souls in our midst. Fearless beings willing to further the collective consciousness by delving into a kaleidoscope of emotions. Embarking upon the greatest adventure ever imagined into the sacred, hallowed jungles of time and space where illumination is taken to dazzling new levels and salvation guaranteed. *Not for what they might do with their lives,* but for simply seeing them through. The Bon Voyage parties.

We owe you BIG.

If you just start dancing

I can *assure* you, by the powers vested in me (more than you could ever imagine), the music will be added. As will the partners, the giant disco ball, and whatever else you like.

But I must warn you, "start", is not to be confused with "start, and then stop to see if anything happens". Nope, that's "I'm scared, tired, and not sure what I really want."

I mean "start", as in "never stop, never look back, because even if I've made a 'mistake', at least I still get to dance."

Do your thing, and I'll do mine.

Cha, cha, cha.

If you know what you want,

and you can remember that "thoughts becoming things" is the *only* law at play in time and space, what else matters, but what you choose to think today?

Bonsai!

Believe it or not,

if it weren't for your so called issues, problems and challenges, there'd be no other way you could become even happier, cooler, and more enlightened than you have ever been before.

Granted, you, being even cooler, boggles the mind.

I keep telling 'em

that it's a jungle out there; that time and space isn't a place for "scaredies"; that toes are stubbed, hearts are broken, and dreams are sometimes shattered into a million pieces. I tell 'em that the illusions are so captivating they won't even remember who they really are. And that the emotions can be so painful, at times they might wish they were dead.

But it's like, that just makes them want to go even more.

Adventurers.

You bad.

What part of "visualize"
do you think most people misunderstand?

Or don't they do it, just once a day, for 5 minutes a day, because they've yet to realize that *whatever it is* they *most want* lies only a little thinking away?

"Can you hear me now?"

Just once a day, for 5 minutes a day, followed by a little "preparing the way", and you, too, could sing like Madonna, golf like Tiger, and waltz like Matilda.

Sometimes, when it seems
your wings have suddenly and unexpectedly been clipped, maybe, just maybe, there's more to learn by staying where you are.

Maybe not.

You decide.

You know that feeling,

when all of a sudden it seems like everything you ever wanted to happen, starts happening at once. And you're totally blown away, on top of the world, almost feeling like you don't even have any more dreams because they're all coming true. Yet you're slammed because you're stretching yourself like you've never stretched before just trying to keep up with them. And everyday some new magical realization hits you! And you've never felt so happy in your life. Except that you wish so badly that everyone close to you could have the same overwhelming experiences; the same sensory overload. And more, you wish everyone on the planet could feel it too, at least just a little, because it's so intoxicating. And you feel like you now understand all the tough times, and all the slow days, and all the phases when it seemed like absolutely nothing was happening in your life. And you wonder why you haven't always felt like this because what you feel is so much more than just the joy of dreams coming true. It's like you're feeling the heartbeat of everyone's life at once.

And you realize there's always been so much more to be happy about, than sad. And you wonder what it was that used to trouble you, and how it could have seemed so real, or how it could've seemed bigger than the beauty you now face. And you just shake your head, knowing how perfect everything is. How perfect it's always been, and how perfect it will always be. And you give thanks with your hands over face, tasting the salt of your tears, and you know that this, this feeling, more than anything else you've ever experienced, was so meant to be?

Well, this is just a tiny, little taste of what it feels like to be the Universe, at all times.

Sure I cry. Whenever you do.

It's one kind of victory

to slay a beast, move a mountain, and cross a
chasm. But it's another kind altogether to realize
that the beast and the mountain and the chasm
were of your own design.

Jambo!

Well, by this point in the day, if my calculations are correct, I expect you've already begun thinking of yourself as "mere mortal". Somewhat alone, a little bit confused, and responsible for figuring out how to make your life take-off.

So... just thought I'd send you a reminder that at this very moment, there are a million eyes upon you, grateful for your courage. That you *already* know, all you need to know. And that whether or not you can see it, you're already soaring.

Bravo.

Go ahead, want it all.
Just learn to be happy before it arrives, or you may not notice when it does.

Hurry, it won't be long!

Whatever you're going

to do today, please, do it to the best of your ability. As if it was all the mattered; as if it was all you had; and as if your very happiness depended upon it. Because these are among the very truths you came here to learn.

Funny... If you were to repeat

the following phrase every single hour on the hour, or even, just once, every single day, for months or years, what do you think would eventually happen?

"I'm so sleepy, I'm just so tired, it's all I can do to stay awake..."

I know, I know, you're way beyond this. But, here's a twist: What if, while bright-eyed and wide-awake, feeling like you were in the best shape of your life, brimming with vitality, you began with the above mantra, what would happen then?

Okay, okay, so you're an old soul. But, what if these things weren't said while in a deep, meditative state, in an absolutely quiet room, with no distractions or daydreaming? Would the results still be debilitating?

All right, Guru, I think I'm about to "get" you, but first one more tease.

What if you didn't read another book on the "nature of reality"? Didn't bother to hire a therapist? Or follow a role model?

And you totally blew off the concepts of practicing, discipline, and sacrifice? Would your sleepy mantra still have any affect on you?

Oh my, I think I've done it. Have you ever before realized how ridiculously easy it is to transform your life? That no matter how poor you are today, nor how in debt, or how bruised and tattered, nor how unhealthy, or how lost, or how lonely... you already possess all the power, wisdom, and ex-perience necessary to begin radically transforming your life by wisely choosing the words you speak, in spite of all evidence to the contrary?

Tallyho, abundant, triumphant and happy soul,

Yeah, yeah, I know, I know you weren't born yesterday. And now you know, that you "feel like a million bucks", that everything you "touch turns to gold", that you always "say the right thing at the right time", that "life is easy and fun", that your "path is clear", and that you know exactly "what to do" even if you can't yet "see" it.

You couldn't be more loved
than you are right now.

There are no challenges,

issues, or crises that do not contain within them
seeds of opportunity that could not have
otherwise existed.

Bet you didn't know how lucky you were!

It's wise not to ask others,

not even me, for much of anything - guidance, help,
time, comfort, security, friendship, compassion,
trust, respect, money, love - that you yourself
would not give.

Just a silly waste of time.

Give what you most want.

A Manifestation Tip
from your friend, the Universe

Feeling gratitude in advance, before you even receive, as if you already had, whether for direction or abundance or anything else, opens the floodgates.

Did you catch the emphasis on feeling?

Ain't it grand?

You know, all the people, millions and millions and millions, who have gorgeous bodies that fill them with pride. Who've created enormous wealth - more than they could ever spend. Who have loving friends scattered all over the globe. And most have no more intelligence than a gopher.

They just didn't take "no" for an answer.

Think about it.

From a big-time gopher lover,
The Universe

Of course it's hard at first.

It's always hard at first. You're going where you've never gone before in the jungles of time and space. Cutting and hacking and slicing your way through the thick, clinging bush.

And though the scenery may seem like it never changes, the day will come when from high on a new plateau, you'll look back in *total awe* - amazed at the distance covered, the perils faced, and the heights attained. Overcome by the inevitability of it all, bursting with pride, and struck most by the realization that the only true dangers you ever faced were during the times you felt like giving up or settling for less.

Awh, awh-WAAAA, AWH-wahhhhhhhhhh,
The Universe

And you're also gonna laugh like a hyena when you see the tigers were made of paper and the lions were only me.

Did you like my Tarzan

impersonation yesterday? He taught me himself! I
love, love, love impersonations. I do a great Jane,
too. You'd never know it wasn't really her,
believe me.

Actually, there isn't a soul on the planet that I
haven't "done". And when I say "done", I mean,
"hang ten, all out, the Full Monty". Sometimes I get
so carried away that I actually forget I'm the
Universe! I *hate* when that happens. Quite the
juxtaposition, if you can picture it. In one moment
I'm the Alpha and the Omega, and everything in
between. And in the next I'm yearning and pining
for my own fabulous house, and dreaming
poetically that one day, yes, one day, just maybe, if
I work hard enough, if I'm good enough, if I'm not
asking for too much, and if it's right for all
concerned, my dreams will come true.
Can you imagine? *Me?*

Get my drift?

There are no finish lines in life,

yet perpetually seeking them, in terms of the quick fix, the big win, or a home run, serves only to remind you of what's missing, reinforcing the imagined lack. However, when one stops looking for results and embraces the journey as it is, the days will soon be innumerable when, looking back, you marvel at the distance covered.

Hi-Ho, Silver...

It only seems to take a long time when you're looking for finish lines, Kemosabi.

In your wildest dreams,

did you ever expect it would seem so real? That your pains and sorrows would cut so deep, and that your joys and laughter would feel so sublime?

No, I didn't think so, because one can't know, until they go, which is why you're there. To feel the emotions that can only be known by immersing yourself into the illusions of have and have not. Because in time and space, no matter how much you have, there's always more, and no matter how much you lack, there's always less. Therefore by simply being there, no matter what you do, nor who you become, nor how much you think you gain or lose, your purpose will be achieved.

To the winner's circle.

The slate is otherwise blank, your thoughts, still, invariably become the things and events of your life. And just as much can be learned by living in wealth and abundance, as without... So, let's do wealth and abundance.

It's like there are countless

rooms in the mansion of your mind. Some lavishly appointed and others quite Spartan. Rooms bursting with their own creative energy that draw you into action. And others that make you feel frightened, or angry, or resentful the moment you've entered them. There are rooms that inspire hope and foster new relationships. And others filled with memories of what's already come to pass and of dreams that never did.

And it's like the more time you spend in any given room, gazing from its windows, the more the outside world begins to justify, reinforce, and in every case, *resemble it.*

And it's like most people just think they find themselves, at any given point in a day, in one room or another without ever realizing that every second of every day, they consciously choose which room to hang out in.

Really, dear, it is your house... But just a fig leaf?

Persistence,

persistence, persistence.

On the surface it might just seem like physical flailing, but spiritually, you're speaking directly to me and you're saying, "You hear me, and you hear me good! There ain't no way I'm doing without. I *refuse* to accept "maybe", "sort of", or "not yet". I *am* the power, the glory, and the way. My words quicken the ether, my actions fulfill their prophecy, and thy Kingdom come on earth, as it is in heaven... Pa-rum-pum-pum-pum."

And frankly, when confronted with such clarity. Such style. Such finesse. It makes my knees go wobbly and I'm like putty in your hands.

Rock on, rock on.

You're freakin' me out!

I can't remember when you last looked so radiant. When your inner beauty shone so bright. When your step was so light and your smile so heavenly. And it's Monday! What's gotten into you?!

Does this have anything to do with recalling your divinity? Have you realized that time truly is on your side, and that more than enough of it remains for us to do your greatest work? Is it that you now see how much you already have, how many you've already helped, and how much you've already done?

Ah-ha! Your eyes just did that sparkly thing, again. Moon beams just shot from your finger tips. The aroma, all around you, is like lavender. And all your angels are locked wing to wing singing, "We-e-e-e-e are the champions..."

Okay, okay... I pulled your leg a little there. Truth be told, I can't remember when you didn't look like this. All together now...

Don't you love "Queen"?

You know what's kind of wild?

It's kind of wild that suddenly, at this very crossroads of time and space more than ever before there are so many billions of people yearning to awaken and understand the truth about themselves, their divinity, and the magic.

You know what else is kind of wild? Just as this need arose, simultaneously, all over the world, there have appeared the greatest teachers, though in far smaller numbers, who have ever graced your plane. Those who are actually living these truths, leading with the example of their lives, and healing those in need through simple conversation.

Anyway, want to know what's even more unbelievable? That you sometimes consider yourself more of the student.

Nope, don't worry, it hasn't affected your performance. You're already a legend.

Do you think gravity

has to work twice as hard to hold an elephant to the ground, as it does an acorn?

Ha.

So please understand, it's the same with the principle of thoughts becoming things. The size of your dreams has *nothing* to do with the likelihood of them coming to pass, *nothing*.

Think BIG.

If I were a business professor
and you were my student, today's lesson
might sound like this:

Class... class... CL-A-A-A-S-S!!

In the "real" world, it's better to have loved and
lost, tried and failed, dreamed and missed, than to
sit out your turn in fear. Because the loss, the
failure, and the miss, however painful, are like
temporary market adjustments, soon forgotten.
Whereas the love, the adventure, and the dream,
are like investments that for the rest of your life
and beyond, never stop paying dividends.

Now, who brought me an apple?

Dr. Love

*Right you are! "How can you lose something you're still
capable of giving? How can you fail if you haven't
stopped trying? And how can you miss, as long as your
still aiming?" One Gold Star on the forehead coming
up, except... Someone misspelled "you're", again.
Oh, what a shame.*

Hoping, wishing and praying
shouldn't ever be confused with *doing*.

Know what I mean?

As in, doing "all you can, with what you've got, from where you are".

Hup! Stop! No! No! No!

Thinking about "how", weren't you? How you're going to get from "here to there" kind-of-thoughts. The cursed how's. Bummer, huh?

There's nothing quite as demoralizing in the human experience as trying to use your brain to map the unseen, because immediately you sense it's hopeless... a*nd you're right!*

You can't map the unseen! But *I* can.

You just need to define "there" and get busy doing what you can in *every* direction that feels right, though insisting upon none. Do the logical things (like knocking on doors and turning over stones). Do the spiritual things (like visualizing and taking catnaps). And leave the accidents, coincidences, and spontaneous illumination up to me.

In a way it's almost like throwing paint on the wall, and then trusting me to connect the dots. Because I will, and the resulting masterpiece will *blow you away*. Promise.

After all, who do you think gave the
"Mona Lisa" her smile anyway?

Whoohoooooo! Great news!

Everything, absolutely everything you've ever
wanted, now lies within reach!

Of course... you still have to reach.

*Hey, you have to admit, that's a pretty
small price for everything.*

Dreams are like that...

Most of the time you don't even know how close
you are, until *after* they've come true.

Sometimes, even, the very day before they come
true, it still feels like they're a million miles away.

Something to remember.

*I think it works like this because if you knew how close
you really were, you'd probably get so nervous that
your legs would shake, your voice would break, and
you'd come so undone that we'd have to call
for a "do-over".*

The easiest way
to avoid let-downs and disappointments, is...

No, it's not lowering your standards.
That's quitting.

No, it's not releasing expectations.
That's an old wives' tale.

And no, it's not relinquishing all mortal desires.
That's an Oriental religion.

It's never tricking yourself into thinking that your
happiness is dependant upon the things and events
of time and space, or what other people think,
say and do.

*And no, it's never really had anything to do with
chocolate. That was The Cookie Monster.*

Just because all things
are possible, doesn't mean you're
supposed to do all things.

*Besides, it's not as if you weren't
going to live forever.*

Do it *your* way
and you'll win the attention, and the respect,
of the whole world.

Not that you need it.

Ever wonder how much patience

you should have with someone, you know, before
you lose your temper?

Infinite.

But careful now. That doesn't mean you have to
wait for them, stay with them, or hang around
them. Lord, no. It just means that for as long as
you choose to keep them in your life,
understanding them, not changing
them, is everything.

You couldn't be freer.

Isn't it strange
how you can find metaphors for life
absolutely everywhere?

I mean, here I sit at Starbucks and everything
seems to be a parody of time and space.

The smiles and warmth that greet you around
every corner, mirror your own.

After you place your order and do what you know
to do, you expectantly trust you'll be served.

Worrying about the hows is ludicrous.

And over at the sidebar, the really sweet stuff...
is free.

*Whoops... There... Right there... Lower... You've got
some foam on the tip of your nose. And yes, we have
Starbucks here. We have everything here.
(First, I might add.)*

Believe me, I know all about it.

I know the stress. I know the frustration. I know the temptations of time and space. We worked this out ahead of time. They're part of the plan. We knew this stuff might happen. Actually, you *insisted* they be triggered whenever you were ready to begin thinking thoughts you've never thought before.

Good on you.

A Community Service Reminder
from the Universe

YOU RULE.

Your gifts are innumerable.
Your insights are profound.
Your choices are endless.
Your touch is healing.
Your thoughts become things.
Your power is indescribable.
And you are loved and adored,
on a moment to moment basis
more than you can now understand.

YOU RULE.

Do you know

what it's going to feel like when the day comes
that everything you now want has come to pass?
When you're living in total abundance, in perfect
health, looking fabulous, with friends and
laughter wherever you go?

It's going to feel like, "Yeah... of course".

That's how well I know you.

Sometimes, not always,

but sometimes, being logical doesn't negate the magic, it stirs it up, because not all miracles hide in the unseen.

Don't be afraid to do the obvious... really well.

Sometimes they even hang around, waiting for you to call, or write, or show up.

It's as if when you move, *I* move.
When you reach, *I* reach. And when you go the extra mile, *I* clear the way... but not one single moment sooner.

Which is why, before you commit, things can sometimes look pretty scary.

"Just like that."

A heartfelt compliment
given for no other reason than because it's
meant, is never, ever forgotten.

You've got the power.

*And that's not just because I move in the lips that
speak them, but also in the ears that hear.*

When the choice is to hurt
or be hurt. Cheat or be cheated.
Violate or be violated.

Always, always, always choose the latter.

Trust me.

Besides, predicaments like these don't just happen.

This might sound a bit conceited,

but there's a part of me that's human, too (if you know what I mean).

I'm a big picture person, and from here I can see all of you. ALL that you've been through, every decision you've ever made, and I know exactly where you're headed. I know your every hope, dream and fear. I've seen you at your "best" and your "worst", on good days and bad. And I gotta confess, I couldn't possibly be prouder of who I've become.

Yeah, me.

So I was thinking...

I know you know that there's the "you" that you know you are - adventurous, good looking, and fun to be around.

And I know you know that there's another part of "you" in the unseen who you've kind of temporarily forgotten - who completes you, loves you, and knows what's really going on.

Well, how'd you like it if I removed the veils? Just for a second? Gave you a glimpse of who that special, divine, otherworldly essence is, so that you might at last begin to comprehend how extraordinary, sublime, and divine you really are?

O.K.... It's me. The entire Universe.

Surprise, surprise, surprise.

What? You were expecting some little Tinkerbell?

It's not a matter of feeling

worthy of love, friends, health, or wealth. Or of appreciating what you already have. Or even of learning to love yourself. These don't have to come first. You don't have to wear a halo to manifest the changes you want.

It's simply a matter of understanding that if you do your part, visualize, prepare the way, and act "as if" without looking back or over your shoulder for quick results, what you want *has to be* added unto you, *as will the feelings* of worthiness, appreciation, and loving your hot-bodied self.

You're pre-qualified to rock the world, there are no others rules.

Besides, feeling unworthy does not make you so.

Anger is one of enlightenment's
many barometers.

Basically, the more you have of one,
the less you have of the other.

Yes-sir-ee-bob.

Don't get mad, get smart.

Do you know

what's already happened this week? A million Beethoven's were born. A million Picassos. A million Einsteins. A million Florence Nightingales. A million Martin Luther Kings. And a million Madame Curies, to name just a few. Each as capable of moving mountains, touching people, and leaving the world far better than they found it.

And so you can just imagine how all of us "here" watch in anticipation to see which ones will have the courage to do whatever little they can each day, with what little they've got, from where they are, before their baby steps turn into giant leaps for all.

It's so in you.

Not desire, but expectation,
unlocks wheels, parts seas, moves mountains,
and changes everything.

To put this tactfully...

If you don't start doing stuff to prepare for all the
fun changes that are about to take place in your
life, *J-e-e-e-e-z*, I just don't know
what might happen.

But I'm darn sure I know what won't.

I'm not from the IRS, but I'm here to help.
I'm also crazy about you!

Oh, yes indeed,

another holiday season is upon you, and it is here, as well, so I bet you're wondering what I'd like as a present. Right?!

Well, since there already is peace on earth (for those who look), since there already is goodwill towards all (mine and yours for starters), and because *you* already live and breathe (took long enough), how about... if I may ask... we talk a little more often? You lean on me a little more often? You expect a few more miracles? And we never stop to look back?

Is that asking too much?

I'm there anyway.

Holy Hanna!

I just realized how few people there are in the world like you. Who have your sense of compassion. Your penetrating insights. And your extraordinary zest for life.
What was I thinking about?

Oh, yeah, my image.

We rock.

Thought it was too much to be coincidence. And while all the rest are in my image, too, somehow not a single one has quite your style and "savoir faire".
H-m-m-m-m...

In the time that it takes you

to read this short *Note*, you could have planted a new image in your mind (anything you like, ideally with an emotional charge), I could have reacted (realigning planets, people, and the sort), and the floodgates would've begun trembling violently as we'd have been drawn *infinitely* closer to manifesting the vision you'd chosen.

Fortunately, there's still time.

It doesn't have to be hard nor take a lot of time. Visualize, it's the least you can do.

One hundred years from now,

it will not matter what your bank account was, what kind of car you drove, nor what style of home you lived in.

On the other hand, since one of the reasons you're in time and space is to understand that you do, indeed, have dominion over all things - nailing these early on would be way cool.

And what better way to be important in the eyes of a child than to <u>live</u> your power, so that they might observe and learn to live theirs?

In life there will always be

challenges that have manifested and dreams that
have not. Yet they'll always pale in comparison to
the number of dreams that have, and
challenges that haven't.

Just look around you.

It's a Wonderful Life,
The Universe

Nice work.

If you know what you want,
if you've made up your mind, if you can see it, feel it, and move towards it in some small way every single day... it has to happen.

You know, I think a big reason
I like the Christmas season so much is because it's one of the few times during the year when masses of people take it upon themselves to "be the difference" in the lives of others, without asking me to do it for them.

Which gives me hope that the day's not far off, when they'll do as much for themselves.

That, and because I really like the "Grandma got run over by a reindeer" song.

To err on the side of generosity,

patience, and kindness... is not to err. Because no little thing slips by the Universe, that isn't returned *bigger and better.*

Changing one's life is easy
and there are lots of ways to go about it, though all exact some sort of price:

Pinpointing invisible, limiting, self-sabotaging beliefs - extremely demanding on brain cells, much easier to do if you have a friend who channels the dead. Either way, it'll keep you busy for the rest of your life.

Discovering what occurrences in the past have mis-programmed you - a therapist can help, though expensive if you don't have insurance, but you can both pretend you're a complex person and that if it wasn't for your childhood, you'd have the perfect life.

Distinguishing between those who really love you and those who wish you harm - super tricky, and may destroy perfectly good relationships. But with a good lawyer you can laugh all the way to the bank while accepting little or no responsibility for your own happiness.

These are just a few of the most popular and widely written about methods. Of course, you could also just begin imagining and moving towards the life of your dreams, treating everyone with kindness, and assuming all is well - profoundly and radically effective for both short and long term gains but totally lacking in drama, requires solo efforts, and is much too easy for most people to take seriously.

Oh well,
The Universe

Hey! I've been looking

over all the holiday photos - the ones I took, of course - and yes, you guessed it, you look absolutely smashing. But honestly, if you don't mind my saying so, you're never quite as beautiful in a photograph - mine or anyone else's - as you are in person. Not even close.

The odd quiver of your lip, the sparkle in your eye, and the hidden question mark, sometimes, when you smile. The confidence behind your laughter, the concern behind your tears, and the unpredict-ability of your wit... The reassurance of your glance, the easiness of your presence, and the "junk in your trunk". I wouldn't change *one single thing*. But you guessed that, too, huh?

Isn't it strange, though, how some still expect to see all that when looking at a photo of themselves, or just staring, motionless, into a mirror?

Maybe if they at least waved, or quivered their lips?

If anyone should ever ask
if you're enlightened...

A L W A Y S S A Y, "Y E S"!

Same goes for being healthy, wealthy, and loved beyond imagination.

Got it?
The Universe

Your word is your wand.

Wow! What an incredible year!

Lots of "first's", ton's of breakthroughs, countless miracles. Stones overturned, doors unlocked, and journeys just begun. It feels like I've waited an eternity for all that's now happening.
(Actually, I have.)

Do you have any idea how many millenniums, billenniums, trillenniums have gone by without you in the world? Thinking the kind of thoughts you now think, doing the kind of stuff you now do, and illuminating all the nooks and crannies (n-o-o-o-o, I didn't almost say crooks and grannies) of the planet I couldn't otherwise reach?

Too many.

Thanks, and Happy New Year!
Your fellow Adventurer,
The Universe

Well worth the wait. But next time I create a reality would you mind, terribly, being among the first to visit?

Whoops...

ever since I began handing out wings and giving dominion to those made in my image, there seems to be the misconception that happiness will come from doing, being, and having it all when actually, as you well know, it's the other way around.

You want to tell 'em?

And, yes. You do have wings.

You know

it seems a shame that for many, life
doesn't seem fair.

But perhaps, that's one of the reasons you were
summoned: to make life a little more bearable for
them until they learn how fair it is, and so that
they can then do the same for others.

So... Did they get a good deal, or what?

And when I say, "perhaps", it's just diplomacy.

What's worse than being human
and hearing fingernails scrape a chalkboard?

Being the Universe and hearing "May I? Can I? Will I?" instead of "Thank you. Thank you. Thank you."

Makes my face squinch up.

I'd even prefer, "Hubba. Hubba. Hubba."

The slate's been wiped clean,
the past has released its grip, and before you sparkles eternity yearning for direction. All that now stands between you and the life of your dreams is just one teeny, tiny, gentle, little rule. Only one condition, prerequisite, principle that matters.

It's not love. It's not God. It's not fate, or luck, or karma. It's not complicated or esoteric, and you needn't sacrifice, plead, or pray to invoke it. It's the only rule that's ever existed, and it's the only one that ever will. No reality can exist in its absence. For its mere existence, you are. With its existence, the power, the light, and the way, are revealed. It's your purpose to discover it, and it's your destiny to master it. It's the beginning, the middle, and the end. The alpha and the omega. The end all and be all of every wish, desire, and dream, and *you* are its keeper.

This caveat of all caveats, is that absolutely nothing can be anything, until it is first imagined. Thoughts become things, *nothing else does*. And so, it's the thoughts you choose from here on out that will become the things and events of your life, forevermore. *It is written in stone*. There's no other way. It's your ticket to anywhere you can dream of. Your passport to abundance, health and friendships. The key to the palace of your wildest dreams.

Your thoughts, and your thoughts alone, will set you in motion. Your thoughts will yield the inspiration, creativity and determination you need. Your thoughts will orchestrate the magic and inspire the Universe. Your thoughts will carry you to the finish line *if you just keep thinking them.* Never give up. Never waiver, doubt or ask. Aim high.

That you've even received this note, that you're able to read it through, means you are so close. So extraordinarily close. The hardest work has been done. The wars have already been waged. The lessons have already been learned. The journey now, is for home.

You're so deserving. You're ready. It's all that stands between you and the life of your dreams.

Let's see, last time I checked

you were still a forever being with as many second chances and new romances saved up as there are stars in the night sky; whose thoughts fly on wings, whose dreams become things, and for whom all the elements bow. (Just in case you were wondering, with the New Year and all.)

Where is it? Where is it?! Have you seen the new year, 2004? I had it just 10 days ago before all the parties and then poof... It... Oh, there it is!

Spinning in the palm of your hand.

Best I can figure

the reason some get down and out, lose
motivation, and watch too much TV, is because
they've somehow forgotten just how *fast* things
can change, and they've yet to discover just
how good they can get.

Even you are going to be surprised.

*Not that I don't check in on Howard Stern
every now and then, myself.*

Of course, the biggest problem
with the "Blame Game", is that everyone loses.

Twister?

Much is said about the lust
for material things, so if I may add to the chorus...
Go for it!

After all, matter is pure spirit,
only more so.

You know how

when you visualize something everyday, to the degree that you can literally *taste* its reality? And you believe in the likelihood of its manifestation with all your heart and soul? And as often as you think of it, in at least some small way, you prepare for its arrival? Yet still absolutely nothing happens?

Right!! That's *impossible*.

Just do your part, I'll do mine, and everything has to change.

Things only get better.

Yeah, I know, not everyone will be ready for that one...
But they're getting better.

Ah-ha!

Do you know what *your* thoughts did last week?!

Oh, yes you do.

They became the things and events of *this* week. The things you thought would be difficult, became difficult; easy, became easy; boring, became boring; and fun, became fun. Where you thought there may be surprises, you were surprised. And where you thought there might be landmines, there were landmines.

Bravo! You can add this week to the list of your most creative accomplishments.

Now, can you guess what your thoughts this week are going to do?

Please, choose every single one of them as if nothing else mattered.

Brace yourself!

It's time for more "good news, bad news".

The good news is that life is just an illusion. A playground of sorts for spiritual adventurers to learn of their divinity. Where absolutely anything can happen, thoughts become things, and dreams do come true. It's like the ultimate test pilot's paradise where they can crash and burn, and do it again. Soar and learn. Rise and fall. Conquer and stall. Or just fly in circles, sometimes on purpose, sometimes not. All while lifting the entire Universe - every imaginable form of consciousness - higher into the light for their tears-and-laughter-bought lessons.

The bad news?

You're the test pilot.

Our hero and ace,
The Universe

Ha, "bad news". You're an unlimited being of light; loved and adored; without beginning or end; invincible, unlimited, almighty... Bad news? I don't think so.

It goes like this...

whatever you're capable of summoning, imagining
and moving towards, however feebly to begin with,
I am capable of delivering.

In expectation,
The Universe

Careful now, 'cause you are gonna get it!

You need never doubt

that I tirelessly conspire on your behalf. Because if it hasn't occurred to you yet, *I need you* as much as you need me. To show me the way, to give me each day, and to go where I couldn't otherwise go.

Amen,
The Universe

You complete me.

No matter what else

you might feel or think, *it's working,* flawlessly,
magically, and without exception. Your thoughts,
beliefs and expectations are the sole cause of the
effects of your life. And while this may give you
pause and have you wonder why you've not yet
met with some of the successes you've sought, let
it also empower you as you remember that the
floodgates *must* fly open and the Kingdom be
revealed at *the precise moment* you release
whatever else you might have felt or
thought about it not working.

There are some folks
who think that life isn't fair, and to them I say,
"Touché!"

Obviously, they see themselves as unlimited Beings of Light for whom all things are possible. They recognize that their thoughts become things, giving rise not only to dreams, but worlds. And they appreciate that their very existence in time and space proves that they're loved
beyond imagination.

Yes, these are the folks who understand that with *dominion over all things*, the cards of life are indeed stacked in their favor.

N'est-ce-pas?
The Universe

You couldn't be more favored.

It's never, never, never,

too late to give thanks in advance for the help you stand in need of, as if you've already received it. Because you just wouldn't believe how much I can accomplish in no time at all, literally.

Thanks for listening.

See? It works.

Scary? You bet it's scary!

Package yourself up into a little ball of energy. Deliberately forget that you're everywhere, always, at once - the sun, the moon, and the stars. Expose yourself, as a tiny baby no less, to the minds of those who are as lost as you - however well meaning. Adopt their beliefs. Play their games. Spend much of your life living by their rules. And trust that you just happen to notice that your thoughts *still*, invariably, without exception, become the things and events of your life. Have faith that you're open minded enough to accept that you're the cause, if you believe in effects; accept responsibility for everything that has, or has not, ever happened to you. So that finally, you recognize your unmitigated super powers, claim them, and *rock the world*!

I'm terrified. It may well be my finest work. How do I follow-up creating a reality like that?

Yes, we'll think of something adventurous.

It *doesn't matter* what "they" do.

Your net worth, net health, and net happiness all hinge *exclusively* upon your net thoughts, net words, and net deeds. Though little can rob you as quickly as thinking that it matters what "they" do.

You've got the power.

How totally cool!
Last night we were dreaming together!

Do you remember? Soaring in and out of mile-high clouds... walking upon lazy lakes and raging rivers... manifesting gold coins from our blue jean pockets... and teaching others how to do the same? Reaching out to the many who are only just now discovering that thriving is their natural state, that abundance is their birthright, and that friends, guides, and admirers are only ever a nod away?

Shoot. You were right. You said you wouldn't remember a thing.

Well, that's OK. I was right, too. I said that those you helped, would never forget. Just like here.

See you tonight,
The Universe

Ain't immortality grand?

Is it just me,
or does *it all* seem far too good
to possibly be true?

*And among other things, how many different flavors
of chocolate does one really need?*

There's *always* a way.

Though chances are, it's not the one that first comes to mind.

Commit only to the end result, drop the "cursed hows",
and be unfettered by closed doors, dashed hopes, and
broken promises.

Your balance of
wit, charm and intelligence...

The measures of your endurance,
strength and stamina...

The depths of your sensitivity,
passion and leanings...

It's *never, not ever,* been done before.

Now, do you think these things were all
proportioned accidentally? Or do you think they
were my idea, designed to take me where
others couldn't?

Bingo.

*Well, yeah, kind of like that new Mars Rover. But on
earth, without the "bugs", and cuter.*

The thing about success,

is that she often arrives at such a late hour that
only the odd balls, freaks, and nuts (you know, the
ones who continued believing, in spite of all
worldly evidence to the contrary) remain
to greet her.

A little weird is good.
The Universe

*Well, she doesn't have to arrive so late, but sometimes
that's also how long it takes before people stop fretting
about whether or not she ever will.*

A Very Special Announcement
to all My People, From the Universe

Owing to the fact that this is a leap month, and a February at that, it has been deemed absolutely necessary to divide all Adventurers up into two groups. The "Very Good Looking Crowd" (VGLCs), and the "Holy-Cow, I Can't Even Believe They're Human Because They're So Gorgeous Crowd" (HCICEBTHBTSGCs).

Further, because this is a non-discriminatory organization, from this day forward both the VGLC's and the HCICEBTHBTSGC's will be treated absolutely identically, without any deviation whatsoever, except - all HCICEB-THBTSGC's will have received today's *Note*, yesterday, approximately 10 hours ahead of schedule.

Should you have received today's *Note*, yesterday (and I happen to know you did, s-h-h-h-h!), please do not tell others who may not have. Nor should you assume that it was just some... you know, programming mistake.

JAMBO!

Now, for the benefit of the VGLS's, here's today's *Note*...

Do you have any idea
of how thoroughly, utterly, and completely *I* want
the very things you now want?

Well, let's just say that after visualizing, and
expecting, and acting with faith, then came you.

We're in this together.

Banzai -
The Universe

May you live ten thousand years!
(As if you haven't already).

Ye-e-e-H-a-a-a! F R I D A Y !

Do you know what that means?

It means you've still got time. It means it's still your turn. It means I can't stop loving you.

xoxo,
The Universe

You haven't mentioned anything to anyone about your status as an HCICEBTHBTSGC, have you?

Ye-e-e-H-a-a-a M O N D A Y !

Do you know what that means?

It means that you're dreaming. In a place where your thoughts become the things and events of your life. And in this dream you're about to manifest, yet again, a brand new adventure framed by the illusion of 7 days. And any villains or heroes you encounter this week; any highs or lows; strikeouts, base hits, or homeruns; Mack Daddies, Sugar Babies, or Oprah Winfreys; will be of your own design.

Ah! If you "do" an Oprah,
please tell her about our Club!

Ye-e-e-H-a-a-a T U E S D A Y !

Just kidding.

A-hem... Even though this will seem like a lie:

No one can be lied to who has not first, somehow, some way, lied to themselves.

Self-deception is really the only kind there is.

There's nothing wrong
with wanting "more".

It means you're alive and well.

Actually, you're "supposed" to want more.

Have you heard the one about
the little boy who asked his mum why
people don't fly?

She told him,
"It's mostly because they forget they have wings."

Sorry, not really funny. But I just didn't want you
to forget about yours.

To the stars,
The Universe

If it wasn't for needing you
there so much, I'd need you here.

"Thanks", on behalf of all those in your life right now who are just too busy, or stressed, or sad, to see how much you add to theirs.
(You know who I mean.)

Hope you had a fabulous Valentine's weekend,
The Universe

I'm not wild about cloning,
unless they're talking about you.

Rule #1 for Giving:

Expect not that your Kingdom will come, nor your
bounty be multiplied, via the recipient
of your kindness.

Drives me absolutely, totally crazy - and severely
limits my options.

Besides, I've always preferred surprising you.

If you only knew how many

miracles you've already performed, nothing would
ever again overwhelm you, frighten you, nor
seem impossible.

And you'd begin admiring yourself,
as we always have.

Just a word from you,
just a word - and I'm there.

No matter where "there" is. No matter what you want. No matter what you need. No matter where you've been. No matter where you're headed. No matter when you ask. No matter how you ask. No matter who's there with you. No matter who else you're thinking of. No matter what, no matter what, no matter what.

Please, believe me,
The Universe

And I travel with all the angels - every single one of them - with just a word from you.

Of course dreams come true.

Just look around you. Out the window. Down the
hall. Into a mirror. These were all once
dreams of mine.

And I had a whole lot less to work with.

As you've probably deduced

by now, I don't think in terms of reasonable or unreasonable, likely or unlikely, possible or impossible. I merely figure out the "hows".

Guess what that leaves you with?

Let's give them something to talk about.

You have a track record here,
have you forgotten?

Little... teensy... tiny... That's how all of your present issues, challenges and so called problems will one day soon appear.

And then you'll wonder - one hot summer's eve as you're floating lazily across your swimming pool (hidden orchestra playing loudly in the background), healthy, confident, and just beaming about your recent successes in real estate; toned, sculpted, and tanned, carelessly splashing your friends, telling jokes, and occasionally laughing so hard you almost capsize - how you could've ever thought they were such a big deal.

I know you.

You call that thing a bathing suit?

If you were to ask me,

I'd probably say that the #1 cause of loneliness in time and space, is not a lack of friends, but a lack of keeping busy.

I'd even go so far as to say that 9 out of 10 times the solution to every crisis, challenge or problem - in relationships, careers, or otherwise — is to get busy.

Because when you get busy you allow me to slide whatever you most need, be it material, spiritual, or a new friend; answers, ideas or comfort, right under your big ole' nose.

The one time out of ten? It's to first be still -
and then get busy.

Beneath your luminous skin,

just behind the sparkle of your eyes, emanating from the depths of your soul, there's a Fire Breathing Dragon, possessing unimaginable strength, sage wisdom, and thoughts that reach out and sizzle every corner
of the Universe.

A playful dragon. A fearless dragon. A good looking dragon. Colossal, yet swift; spontaneous, yet clever; unreasonable, yet measured; outrageous, yet innocent; determined, yet patient; cautious, yet carefree; light, yet less filling.

A predator, guardian, and connoisseur
of adventure.

And I think it's really cool how, lately, I'm seeing more and more of it come out.

Gives new meaning to "hottie" - huh?

Bagnnn... Bagnnnn... Bagnnnn...

We interrupt your day with a test, a test of *the* Emergency Broadcast System.

Can you see me, right now?

Yes... I'm the light, and all it shines on.

Can you hear me?

Yep - every single sound, and the silence, too.

Can you feel me? Right now? In the air on your skin, under your feet, and in the palms of your hands. The tugs at your heart, the rhythm it keeps, and the blood in your veins?

Right. Now next time you have cause for alarm, see me. Next time you need absolutely anything, listen to me. And next time you feel all alone, remember you're not.

Once you make up your mind

and start something, commit to it, say "*Yes!*", and never look back. Do you have any doubt, *any whatsoever*, that I will not rush to your side?

That legions won't be summoned? That players won't be drawn to your corner? Connections made? Circumstances crafted? Dots connected?

That the course of history won't be irrevocably changed?

Good, I didn't think so.

I'd say you're ready.

Was that a "Yes!"?

Oh, shoot!

Did I remember to ask you to turn off the lights?
You know, in the "Hall of Records" after I showed
you where all the books written about you were?

Remember, not a word to anyone! (Most don't
believe in traversing time, yet, and they'll think
you're whacked.)

S-h-h-h-h...
The Universe

Told you. You put on quite a show, didn't you?
Changed the bloomin' world.

Persistence is priceless,
but its value lies in doing, doing, doing, not in
waiting, waiting, waiting.

OK? OK? OK?
The Universe

*Not that you were hanging around for someone,
someway, or somehow!*

It totally flips me out.

People talk to me, they ask me stuff, they show me things, yet so rarely do they ever expect a reply.

Am I invisible, or something?

Well, enlightenment
is kind of like flying for the first time
without wings.

Of course, there's the exhilaration, the happiness,
and the intoxicating sense of freedom that's
almost indescribable.

But there's also the subtle shock at what you now
see as the inevitability of your accomplishment.
The wonderment of how you hadn't seen this so
clearly before mingled with acceptance. And the
dim recognition that it's part of some distant
agreement you obviously partook of.

And at last, as you come to your senses and finally
think to gaze below upon the tiny jewel you've
called home for so long, you're struck with a jolt
as you see it so magically and effortlessly
suspended – *floating* – in space, and you realize for
the first time, that even there you were
flying all along.

Up ahead!!! There's a tree coming right at you!

You know those feelings of

euphoria, excitement, and inspiration that send your spirit soaring?

Well, they're just me and all the angels, finally rushing through one of the many doors you've knocked upon, down the hall, and dancing into the light of your searching heart.

And those feelings of depression, sadness, and powerlessness that make you feel like you're carrying the weight of the world on your shoulders?

They're us, too. Reminding you that there are still a few more doors to try.

Let's get this party started.

When it comes to "having it all",

many fine, young souls take issue with the word, "have". They're concerned about the concept of ownership. Their soul is taunted by a guilt for the pleasure it derives from material things. And they quiver at the thought of "others" having less than them.

Of course, such righteous and selfless thoughts are a significant contributor to the creation of lack in a world of endless abundance, but they'll learn.

"Kids...!"

Actually, if it were any easier,
it wouldn't be worth it.

You'll see.

Do you think having your own

private, little planet where you could have, do and be anything you dreamed of, with as many friends as you chose, would be worth it, if the price of admission was to forget how you got there so that you could discover your throne, on your own?

All bow.

You always were a trendsetter. But do you have any idea how many others I've had to strike the same bargain with?

Whoo-hoo!

The script for the most *amazing* time in your life is
nearing perfection! We're so excited and happy
for you. Bravo. Bravo. Bravo.

It's complete with friends and laughter, wealth and
abundance, health and harmony. And best of all,
there are going to be some really neat surprises.
BIG surprises! Really HUGE, *Texas style.*

And you're gonna say, "B..bu... but... I... I... I...
H... Ho... How? Never in all my life have I imagined
such outrageousness! All my expectations have
been exceeded! *Never* have I dreamed of being so
blessed!" And we're gonna say, "Oh, yes you did."

And you're gonna say, "Oh, no I didn't".

And we'll say, "Did".

And you'll say, "Didn't."

And then we'll remind you of those occasions
when you simply saw yourself happy. Visualizing
euphoric happiness, bypassing the details. Smiling
from ear to ear in your mind's eye, pumping your

fist, dialing your friends' cell phone numbers with shaking fingers, happy tears running down your face, *when you left all of the "hows" to the Universe.*

And you're gonna say, "Oh."

And we're gonna say, through tears of our own, "Nice hows', huh?"

"Action!"

Have you ever thought of writing for the movies?

One more thought on the "hows":

Just because you're not to mess with them, doesn't mean you don't get busy doing all you can, with what you've got, from where you are.

The difference is in how you see what you do: you don't do all you can with an eye to hitting a home run, but with an understanding that for each door you knock upon and every stone you turn over, you're pitching the ball to me.

The more balls you pitch, the greater my options, and the further it will sail.

Batter up,
The Universe

It's like, if you want me to do ALL I can (move mountains and that sort of thing), you must do ALL you can (cast your bread, sort of thing).

How to make anything happen...

Act as if it already has, and never look back.

Thanks for being there,
even through the "hard" times.

And sorry if they've ever seemed like too much.
But I'm pretty sure it was you, after all, who said,
"I want it *all* - no matter the cost."

You power shopper, you -
The Universe

For just a moment,

can you imagine that on the day the earth was created, I'd want to experience her in every imaginable form?

Good.

Now can you imagine that when it came to creating the animals, I couldn't just pick one - but would want to soar through the skies, swim in the oceans, and burrow in the fields?

Excellent. I had to be all of her animals, to experience all of their secrets.

So when it came to having dominion over all things, it must now be just as obvious that I had to *be* everyone.

And I am.

I walk in your shoes. Everyday.

Do you remember

way back when, on the day you first earned your wings, how you worried about whether or not you'd be able to use them to lift yourself, and thereby the entire planet, higher?

And so I reminded you that the reason you earned them was because you already had?

You've already earned all that your heart desires. Besides, you didn't really think with all the encrusted diamonds, inlaid pearls and the monogrammed gold flaps you special-ordered, they were really about flying even higher, did you? I don't even know how you walk around with them things. But I'm proud as can be.

Of course it's true

everyone's born with a gift. One that will allow them to fill a special place in the Universe that absolutely no one else can fill. A blessing that makes all other blessings pale in comparison. A gift of incalculable value to the entire world when it's uncovered, explored and embraced.

Yours?

Being you.

WOW, you must have known someone really "high up"!

Universal Personality Test

Want to know how to tell whether you were born with the gift to heal? Or perhaps if your strengths lie in leadership? If you're a left or right "brained" individual? Whether or not you're truly a "people person"? Whether or not, given your beliefs, friends, laughter, and abundance will flow to you effortlessly, or should be diligently sought after?

Just decide.

It's always worked before.

The adulation. The worship.
The glory. The throngs. The masses. The fans.

You'd think by now the novelty would have worn off - but those few (and I do mean, few, by our standards) who are brave enough to adventure into the jungles of time and space, have our deepest admiration.

Because even as we know that wherever they find themselves nothing will be as it seems; that no matter what happens, they'll always be safe and protected; and that their inevitable homecoming celebration will make the Academy Awards look like a McDonalds' Happy Meal, they know none of this. And so the heights of their glory and the depths of their despair have become legend in a land of legends.

And you thought "Reality TV" was popular.

I'm hungry!

Hungry for adventure.

The adventure of love.

Tell you what: The more of it you give today to the least deserving on your list, the more your life will change.

Oh, they love me all right!
They really, really love me.

But sometimes I wonder if the reason they love me has anything to do with the thought that one day, just maybe, I'm going to be the spark, ignite the fire and summon the magic that will make all of their dreams come true?

Yikes, are they ever going to be surprised when they find out that's their job?

Have you heard about the
"Bewitching Hour"?

Actually, it's top secret so I'll whisper.

Every single morning, ever since time began, before the sun even rises, the drums start beating, the choirs start singing, the energy starts rising and every single soul who has ever lived clamors around the plane of manifestation as a chanting begins... And gets louder and louder... And goes faster and faster until... a feverish pitch is reached and the celestial skies part with a clap of thunder, revealing billions upon billions of the most beautiful angels you have ever seen. Flying down from the heavens, some with wings outstretched, others with theirs pointed back. Darting, diving, banking and rolling - some so fast they're only a blur - while others seem to float by as if catching what remained of a mid-summer night's breeze. Every one of them a reflection of the greatest, the loveliest, and the highest I've ever imagined. Every one of them a messenger of hope, and peace, and joy; healers and teachers, comforters and creators. And every one of them about to greet a brand new day in time and space with a morning yawn, sleepy eyes, and the power to ROCK THE WORLD.

This is the "Bewitching Hour". Shhhh...

And if you listen real hard, you can still hear the drums.

Hosanna in the highest.

Nice inverted-triple-axle-gallactica this morning. Seems like just yesterday when you were still somersaulting the whole way - doesn't it?

Oh, hi...

at least *you* are still talking to me. Was just sitting here on the beach wondering whether or not the whole thing was a good idea in the first place, you know?

When the idea first dawned on me, it just seemed like one heck of an adventure. Endless possibilities. Incomparable camaraderie. A little bit of me in everyone (OK, a lot). My style, my rhythm, my appetite for fun.

I had no idea people could feel so lost... So sad... So alone.

Well, this much I know for sure: next time I throw a "bring-your-out-of-body" party in the middle of the night, we won't turn off the music at the sound of the first alarm clock. Escorts will be provided upon re-entry to avoid accidental body swapping. And illumination, guardianship, and inspiration shall be made available at all times for those confused, *just like on earth*, as long as they ask and expect to be heard.

Shake your tail feathas...
The Universe

What did you think I was talking about? By the way, loved your kilt. Where it fit.

If you ever find yourself driving

down the motorway of life looking for an exit that
says "Easy Street", may I remind you that that's
where you got on, following a sign that said,
"Paradise, this way. Road under construction.
Watch out for "light workers", falling debris, pot
holes, and slippery patches. No turning back."

And you said, "Cool".

What do you mean, "Are we there yet?"
You're now one of the light workers.

I should have shared this earlier

but, well, I'm the Universe and I've been busy.

In the beginning, long before there were even
beaches to walk along, clouds to float upon, or
stars to wish on, I dreamed of you and
your happiness. And everything that has
ever been added since was to that end.

*See? You are so much more to me than
just pretty planet decoration.*

Rising suns and babbling brooks.

Tropical forests and sleeping meadows.

Modern marvels and breakthrough sciences.

Exciting discoveries and limitless frontiers.

Devoted friends and caring strangers.

Lives and loves and souls to hold, so close,
one's own heart could burst.

Look at it like this: It's not so much that you have
to wait for your dreams to come true, but that
you get to - in a Garden of Eden, a paradise of
paradises, in the palm of my hand.

Can you even count the splendors?

Here's a little "Inevitability Test"

to check on the progress you're making towards achieving any particular dream.

You're pretty much doing something about it, every single day.

Yes, visualizing counts. But preparing the way counts twice. And acting "as if" it's a done deal, seven times.

An enlightened soul

is not one to whom truth has been revealed, but
one who has summoned it. And not just when
they've been driven by pain, but when life's
seas were as calm as glass.

But, you have to admit it's kind of handy that way,
pain. Just worked out like that. Honest.

Of all the luck!

Can you believe it?

You. In paradise. Now. Exactly as you are.
Exactly as it is.

Do you have any idea how many souls in the
unseen wish they could be in your shoes? Who
wish they could see through your eyes? Who wish
they could feel what moves in your heart? Have
your friends? Share your loves? Face your fears
and your beasts?

Oh, heck yeah, your fears and your beasts! Are
you kidding? Especially your fears and your beasts!
Because from where they are, it's so much easier
to see how soon they will pass, how triumphant
you will be, and how much more they'll
make possible.

To them, it's like every day is your birthday.

Haven't you always
found your way?

Hasn't there always been a light in the darkness? Haven't you always gotten back up? Haven't there always been serendipitous surprises, unexpected twists, and triumphant comebacks? And, haven't you always had someone to love? Not to mention all of your dreams that have already come true.

Coincidences? Or maybe, do you think, you, too, have always been loved?

April, what a cool month.

Thursday, what a cool day.

Thoughts, still manifesting, as predictably
as the tides rise.

You, still as free to choose those thoughts,
as the wind blows.

Seems all is well in paradise.

Anything else I can do for you, anything at all?

Love,
The Universe

*Yeah, right. Sorry. As if something could beat April,
Thursday, and the power to have it all. Guess I'm just
in one of those silly moods. xxoo*

Think not that today foretells
tomorrow, for it never has.

Same goes for the past.

Only you can do that.

Never forget,

the scorecard that matters most is invisible, and won't be seen by others until the game is over. At which point, it'll be distributed via our version of hi-def broadband, in 3D Technicolor to everyone you've ever known, and then some.

Of course, all the check boxes will be blank, except for where you might want to rate yourself (highly discouraged, by the way), but still, every single fear you ever faced, every bridge you ever crossed, and every life you ever touched, will be known and celebrated by all.

Actually, the party's already started, but it gets a little bigger every day as the ripples created by your kindness and courage spread further and further.

Hey, you're HUGE in the unseen.

It isn't easy at first,

but one of the greatest gifts you could ever give someone who makes your heart soar, is the freedom to learn their own lessons, at their own pace.

Even trickier, is discovering that one of the greatest gifts you could ever give someone who gets on your nerves, is the freedom to learn their own lessons, at their own pace.

And perhaps most challenging of all, is understanding that one of the greatest gifts you could ever give yourself, is understanding that your heart soaring and your nerves fraying, have never been dependant upon other people and their lessons.

In all cases, I meant, "besides chocolate".

As much as I love my "job",

I do have "my days".

Maybe you can help me out?

Tell me, what advice would you give a child who came to you asking what their favorite color should be?

To follow their heart? That no color is right or wrong? That if they wanted to, they could always change their mind later, any number of times? That their happiness with their choice is all that matters? Not to give it too much importance? That they don't have to decide at all? That you approve no matter what they choose?

My, you *are* good!

Now, what if they protested because they heard from friends that there was a special color assigned to them at birth, their soul-color. They felt that a numerology reading might shed some light on their confusion. They wanted confirmation of their choices through a zodiac chart, tea leaves, or a Ouija board. And they asked if finding a new guru would be a good idea.

See?

Sorry to lay that on you. I'm just fishing around for some new answers to the bazillion questions I get each week about careers, loves, and destinies - which to me, from here, are kind of like... crayons.

E-w-w-h-h, nice magenta!

Sure, use all the tools, guides, and helpers you like, I approve of them, too, but maybe, reread the 4th paragraph, above, as well.

Pretend you were me:

You're about to create a new reality. And you know you're gonna hang out there, in every imaginable form, for trillions and trillions and trillions of years.

Do you think, just for yucks, you'd build it in such a way that you might get hurt, become less, or not matter?

Or, as the Universe, the Alpha and the Omega, the bringer of the dawn and each new day, would you be pretty confident that you could craft the most spectacular paradise imaginable? Flawless in every way, yet possessing the odd illusions of pain, loss and your own irrelevance to heighten suspense, enhance the unknown, and make it one unforget-table, spine-tingling, non-stop adventure, that will mean even more to you when you master it again, but from the inside out?

CUT! That's a wrap.

Nice Alpha! Were the purple leotards your idea?

xxoo,
The Universe

PS - Don't believe the illusions.

Have you noticed it, too?
How fears are a lot like highway billboards?

The faster you're moving, the quicker they approach, the larger they get, and the more they block your view of what's real and alive. To the point that they tower above you, larger than life itself, giving you pause and more reason than ever to turn around and retreat to safety.

Yet if you muster the courage to stay the course, in just a blink they're behind you, put into proper perspective. And then as quickly as they appeared, they completely vanish.

If you want to stay the course, then please, just stay the course.

That's why we did away with billboards here a long time ago. Besides, no one uses our highways.

Here's the rub:

If it wasn't so flippin' simple - manifesting change,
finding happiness, living the life of your dreams - I
really do think more people would "get it".

Think, think, and let go.

Release me, release me

to do your will. To move heaven and earth. To orchestrate the players, and summon the circumstances that will change your life completely *by doing your all-out best, with today.*

That's all the leg-up I need.

Basically, if you can *feel* it,
I can deal it.

Whatever you want.

With compliments,
The Universe

Emotion summons circumstances.
The greater the emotion, the greater
the circumstances.

Ever wonder what

the world would be like without you?

Who would shine a light into all the dark corners you now illuminate? Who would comfort, guide, and inspire all those you now reach? Who would smile to those who need yours the most?

We do.

All the time.

And it ain't pretty.

It matters little to so many that you don't even know of your impact. Except, of course, that they wish you did.

Oh, deary, deary me...

So many claim to believe.

So here's what I'm going to start asking them: If you really believed you were guided, wouldn't you begin listening?

And if you really believed you were powerful, wouldn't every true desire be followed by action?

And if you really believed you could provide the spark that makes your dreams come true, wouldn't you stop living as if you weren't sure?

That ought to stir up their coffee, huh?

Let's rock and roll.

Be the miracle.

Through you,
through you, through you...

The magic works through you. Not beside you. Not around you. Not for you. Not instead of you. But through you.

You have to go there. You have to choose your stage. You have to do your dance. Putting yourself in place, to any degree that you can, even if it scares you, even when it's "hard", even if it's just your big toe. Stretch yourself, scoff at the odds, get the ball rolling so that the magic can then come alive and sweep you off your feet with its infinite grace and glory.

You wouldn't just carry around the seeds for the garden of your dreams in your pocket, all the while asking where your flowers were? Nope, you'd have to brave the elements, you'd have to choose the location, and then you'd have to go there.

Your *life* is your wand (or hoe, whatever),
The Universe

There will always be something

else you could have said. There will always be something else you could have done. And there will always be another life you could have lived.

But, frankly, we're still savoring all you *did* say, do, and become, in spite of so many reasons that you might not have.

Yeah, "What would {insert your name here} do?", is part of our pop vernacular now. And you should see your pending endorsement deals! Magic carpets, body wands, pixie dust, the works!

Here's a little trick
to get the ball rolling:

Ask yourself, "What's the most fun I could have
with my life, as it is now, before those big dreams
of mine come true?

Then do it.

A lot.

The next thing you know, those big
dreams will come true.

*And, if you're not even sure what's fun anymore, then
just do anything. A lot. And it will find you.*

It's that simple.

Your thoughts *do* become things. Don't fight it. Don't think there's something else. Don't entertain the false premises of fate, luck, or a God who judges, withholds, or decides. You decide. You manifest. You rule. This is why you're here. This is what you came to discover. To experience your absolute dominion over every flimsy, malleable illusion of time and space. To do, be and have.

Truthfully, it couldn't be any easier. Not any. All you have to do is *think* of what you want, and not deviate from that thought. Which will invariably set you in motion, stir up the magic, and unleash the full force, power and majesty, of a Universe conspiring on your behalf.

Just do it. It's worth everything you've got. Be strong, vigilant and determined, and the Kingdom of Heaven will appear at your very feet.

"I got your back."

Do you know what
you've created?

No, besides an intergallactically known
saunter named after you.

Inspiration, in the eyes that have watched you.
Hope, in the minds that have admired you. And
love, in the hearts that have known you.

Not bad, kiddo, not bad at all.

*But, you might ease up on your sashay
before someone gets hurt.*

Here's some advice for those
who come to you with long faces:

"If you've finally decided, once and for all, to be happy, yet you aren't. Then you haven't yet decided to be happy, once and for all."

Same goes for all the other stuff they've decided.

They're *that* powerful.

OK, just to show I'm still doing all I can to make time and space a happy place, I've decided to make today Friday, yet again!

Now, let's just say

you're a fisher-person, and let's just say that I've rearranged the stars so that this is going to be the luckiest week of your life.

Whoo-hooo...

Tell me, next time you go out on your boat, will you take one pole, or many?

Many. I thought so.

Would you think, maybe for the glimmering of a moment, that as a lucky person you won't have to fish anymore, because the fish will come to you?

No. Probably not. You've always been one of the sharper tools in the shed.

So tell me, why is it so easy for most to see that with luck, even, they still have to put themselves out there, and that the more they do, the greater the yield. Yet when it comes to life's magic, thoughts becoming things, and a Universe conspiring on their behalf, they think their fish will come to them?

Your first mate, always,
The Universe

PS - No, there's no such thing as luck. Just folks who believe in the magic enough to fish at every opportunity.

Don't you marvel at nature?
I do, but then I'm partial.

It holds so many clues about living the life of your dreams, don't you think?

For instance, have you ever seen a momma duck waiting around for her baby ducks to line-up before crossing the street?

Never. Because she knows that the only way her ducks are ever going to line up is if *she* first starts out on a new adventure.

Just one of your ducks,
The Universe

It's the same for your ducks, they won't all line-up either, until you start.

New Soul Orientation

Now, a few words and phrases not in *my* vocabulary: Should. Difficult. Evil. I don't know.

Oh sure, there'll be plenty of times you can use them, and everyone will know exactly what you mean - especially me - at which point all the elements will conspire to make them true for you.

I also never ask "How". Might as well just ask, "What Universe?"

Dismissed,
This Universe

Oh, and there's one more. "Goodbye." It's a bit of fiction that totally tears me up.

Sometimes the suspense here
becomes almost too much.

Like right now.

Before you, in the unseen, there are some
amazing, mind-blowing, circumstances
now brewing.

Wheels are turning, fires are burning, and all
possibilities are being recalculated.

Players, player-ettes, and accomplices are lining up,
soon to burst into your life.

All just waiting for the nod from me...
as I wait for the nod from you.

Wha-Hu-Ha! This is so much fun!

Once you know, commit and never look back.

Best friends may tell you
what to do. Yep, because that's what
best friends do.

Wise friends, however, wouldn't dream of it
because they understand that they'll never know of
all the secrets that stir in your heart, of your gifts
that lie in waiting, nor of the plans that we
have made.

S-h-h-h-h-h,
The Universe

And I'm not telling.

One hundred trillion years!

7 continents!

106 billion people!
(not counting Atlantis, and the others)

96 zillion dreams manifested!

And not once, not even close, not even on my most generous, loving, caring days, has anything ever happened in time and space - good or bad, big or small, rich or poor - that wasn't sparked by someone's imagination followed-up with *their own* baby steps.

Now remind me, what is it you most want?

Not without you,
The Universe

Pssst... Hey, gorgeous!

Want to know a secret?

Everything in your life is a symbol.

A reflection. A clue. A reminder.

Of what you understand, and of what you
don't, made manifest.

Look to the beauty for truth. And to
what hurts, for its beauty.

Oh, yes indeed, life is fair. As fair as it is beautiful.
Though this can't always be seen from too close,
in terms of either time, or space.

Happily...

Between here and there, the *only* thing that matters is what you think between now and then.

The past is simply what you choose to remember, if you even choose to remember it.

Ever pour cement?

Heavy stuff, but it's a simple job. Just mix, set, and leave it alone. You can even make shapes out of it, like ducks, flowers, or figurines, depending on the mold. There's no limit.

Now, let's just say that you don't like the way a particular duck came out. Would you try to re-pour or manipulate the cast concrete, or would you simply start over, considering that cement is dirt-cheap.

Oh, you're way ahead of me! You saw that "mix, set, and leave", was like a metaphor for using your imagination, didn't you? You also got that the mold is your goal or dream. I think the "no limit" tipped you off, too. "Heavy stuff", "simple", and "cheap" were also clues. But what I'm most proud of, is that you saw how re-pouring or manipulating cast concrete is like trying to affect change in one's life by tweaking what's already manifested, instead of going within and manifesting anew.

5 Gold Stars for you today,
The Universe

If you knew of a spectacular

mountain that was very, very tall, yet climbable, and if it was well established that from its peak you could literally see all the love that bathes the world, dance with the angels, and party with the "Gods", would you curse, or celebrate, each step you took as you ascended it?

Right-O. Life is that mountain, and each day a step.

Have no fear. Last time I checked, you were so close to the top they were taking your Toga measurements.

Has it struck you yet

that answers, come before questions? That healing, begins with illness? And that you can't have a dream come true, without a time when it hasn't?

Shoot, isn't it all so perfect? Everyone, no matter where they are on their journey, can be happy.

At all times, and in all matters,
everything is happening in your favor.

Please, don't be afraid.

Not even a little. Not ever. The lions and tigers and bears can't really hurt you. You live in a world of fog and mirrors where there's only the illusion that you could somehow become less than the greatest you've ever imagined yourself to be.

And it's this very image, the highest from within you, that has summoned your boldest dreams. As if by dare, to draw you into the light with their sweet rewards. And as if by chance, to draw you through the very fears that have kept you from it.

Slayer of dragons. Matador of all time and space. Rightful heir to heaven on earth. Don't be afraid. Not even a little.

Amen,
The Universe

I guess I just needed to blog.

You're not here to learn

how to make your thoughts become the things
and events of your life. Too hard, too complicated.
B-o-r-i-i-i-n-g. Leave this to me.

No, you're here to learn that they already do.
Every single one of them. Always have, always will.

How could it be easier?

Imagine yourself

on a warm summer evening before a calm, clear
pond. The moon is full. The stars are shining.
Whippoorwills are whippoor-willing.
And I am with you.

Now, do you know how to float on water? Well,
for the most part you do absolutely nothing, at
which point I can hold you at the surface, in the
palm of my hand. It's simply a matter of physics,
the laws of time and space, and your natural state.

Are you with me?

OK, now you'll have to trust me, but it's the same
when it comes to floating in wealth and abundance,
health and harmony, friends and laughter. These
are your natural state, your default settings, the
"givens" in this great adventure. These are where
true balance is found. They can be yours without
strenuous effort. You don't even have to visualize
them. Just stop the argument that claims you're
without. Surrender in the war that presumes lack.
Come out from the fort that has kept you so
safe, and follow your heart with abandon.

It's as if, when moving

from point "A" to point "B" in your life - from sickness to health, poverty to wealth, whatever - at some point in the journey, arriving at point B becomes inevitable. A sure thing. However, at no point in your journey is this *physically* verifiable - until you reach point "B".

The point being (yuck, yuck), you may have *already* crossed that line. But you'll never know it, unless you see the journey through.

Time and space, what a hoot.

Look to them for answers, direction and meaning,
and they'll rock your world every which way.

Yet discover that they look to you for answers,
direction and meaning, and you will
rock the world.

Take my word for it, the latter is your "ticket".

Tallyho, maestro -
The Universe

What an adventure, if I do say so myself.

Ooh! Ooh! Ooh!

Have I mentioned that everyone knows exactly what you're thinking?

How else could you draw new friends from the unseen? How else would your heroes, heroines, and scoundrels know when to appear, or move on? How else would your "stars" get their cues?

True, they think their own thoughts, too. How else would you know who to cast in each scene?

Just thinking of you, and your power to choose.

Yikes... even those thoughts!

Imagine...

You're sitting upon your throne overlooking your
Kingdom (Queendom, whatever 'dom you like),
and masses upon masses of people surround
you in throngs.

They're cheering your name, laying flowers at your
feet, and imploring you to join them in the village
where they've prepared a feast to celebrate
your life.

You humbly accept their invitation, and
immediately you're whisked off your feet and lifted
high upon the shoulders of your joyful admirers,
thoroughly overwhelmed by their heartfelt
gratitude and desire to please you.

Midway through the most extravagant party you've
ever attended, amid laughter and happy tears, you
begin reflecting on your life and in no way can you
recall what you've done to deserve such an
outpouring of love.

Suddenly embarrassed, and wondering if you aren't
dreaming the whole thing, you turn to a member
of your entourage and whisper in her ear, "Are

you sure there hasn't been some kind of mistake? I mean, I don't even recall having a Kingdom! Who are all these people? Who do they think I am?"

And she whispers back, "There's no mistake. They know exactly who you are. These are just some of the souls whose lives had reached a fork in the road, as most lives do, where hope and despair had met, and because of something you said or did, directly or indirectly - they were, as you might say, shown the way, reborn, and, eventually, they were able to shine their light on to the paths of others in need. That's who they are, and in case you haven't noticed, more keep arriving in a procession that will never end.

"And no, this isn't a dream."

And no, again. I didn't say "thongs".
But I'd imagine that could be arranged.

Everything can change,
so very, very fast.
And it usually does.

Whoo-whoooooooooo!

If it was just about surviving,

getting by, and keeping things the way they are, then how would you explain imagination?

If it was just about sacrifice, selflessness, and altruism, then how would you explain desire?

And if it was just about thinking, reflecting, and spiritual stuff, then how would you explain the physical world?

Get the picture? Want it all.
That's what it, and you, are there for.

Vroom, vroom,
The Universe

You could call me your friend,

but that's not quite enough. You could call me
your guide, but there's more to it than that.

You could call me your conspirator, your helper,
or your agent; your coach, counselor, or confi-
dant; your father, mother, or child. You could call
me the sun, and the moon, and the stars; the wind,
and the sky, and the rain; the past, the present,
and the future.

But really, what I'm getting at, the purpose behind
all these *Notes* and, perhaps what I'd most like to
hear one day, is you calling me "yourself".

O-h-m-m-m-m-m...

Just as I've always called you "myself".
(With unimaginable pride, I might add).

Help spread the word!
A selection of these "Notes" are freely available as e*cards on the Internet at <u>www.tut.com</u> or <u>www.notesfromtheuniverse.com</u>

TUT® Adventurers Club Oath

"In the face of adversity, uncertainty and conflicting sensory information, I hereby pledge to remain ever mindful of the magical, infinite, loving reality I live in. A reality that conspires tirelessly in my favor. I further recognize, that living within space and time, as a Creation amongst my Creations, is the ultimate Adventure, because thoughts become things, dreams come true, and all things remain forever possible. As a Being of Light, I hereby resolve to live, love and be happy, at all costs, no matter what, with reverence and kindness for All. So be it!"

Take the Oath online, at www.tut.com, and begin receiving your FREE, personalized, daily, never-before-published, "Notes from the Universe" by email!

From the Author

If ever there was proof of magic in my life, the fact that I now spend part of every day writing for "the Universe", is it. As the year 2000 dawned, just after we had closed the last of our TUT stores and liquidated our remaining inventory, I briefly hit the pavement with my accountant's resume in hand.

Fortunately, no one was hiring (at least not me!), and fortunately again, I had enough money from our T-shirt days to coast awhile. Even more fortunately, I still had a thousand or so people looking forward to receiving my free "Monday Morning Motivators" via email each week.

So I decided that as long as I didn't have to work, yet, I'd keep doing the one thing that filled me with the greatest sense of accomplishment and purpose - write. And figure out how to make it pay, later.

Talk about scary. As the months rolled by, there were plenty of nights I tossed, literally in a sweat, thinking "*what* am I doing with my life? How did I get here? What went wrong? What if I don't make any money at this? What if I have to sell my home? What if I can't find a job, and no one will buy my home? What if? What if? What if...?" And day after day, week after week, month after month, my reserves dwindled and *nothing* came in.

But I knew a trick. I knew that figuring out "the hows", wasn't really my job, they belonged to the Universe. I also knew to focus on the end result, the kind of life I wanted, and to get busy turning over every stone, knocking on every door, following every impulse, so that theoretically, at least, the Universe could take care of the details.

Whaaaaa! Has it ever!!! Somehow, during all the knocking and turning and visualizing, I acted on enough hunches and instincts to keep me buoyed with the necessary optimism to press on and not look back. And literally, the next thing I knew, the Adventurers Club was born and the Universe began using email. At last count, solely from word-of-mouth advertising, 33,267 people in 146 countries are signed up. Today, I look around and can hardly believe the reversal and rise of my good fortune.

I always knew it worked, but the thrill of experiencing it yet again, in spite of my worries, doubts, and frustrations, has been an awesome adventure; one I know *everyone* deserves and can experience for themselves.

If nothing else, please remember, no matter how dark things get, no matter how difficult, if you continue to do your part, the Universe has to do its part - it's the law, and things will turn around.

To the life of *your* dreams,

TOTALLY UNIQUE THOUGHTS®

...because thoughts become things!®

Launched in 1989 by 2 brothers and their cool mom, TUT® believes that everyone's special, that every life is meaningful, and that we're all here to learn that dreams really do come true.

We also believe that "thoughts become things®", and that imagination is the gift that can bring love, health, abundance and happiness into our lives.

Totally Unique Thoughts®
TUT® Enterprises, Inc.
Orlando, Florida
www.tut.com
USA